THE
POWER OF
Me

6 POWER TOPICS THAT WILL HELP
YOU DISCOVER YOUR TRUE SELF

TISHA LANKAMP, MA, CLC

Balboa Press books may be ordered through booksellers or by contacting:

Balboa Press
A Division of Hay House
1663 Liberty Drive
Bloomington, IN 47403
www.balboapress.com
844-682-1282

Because of the dynamic nature of the Internet, any web addresses or links contained in this book may have changed since publication and may no longer be valid. The views expressed in this work are solely those of the author and do not necessarily reflect the views of the publisher, and the publisher hereby disclaims any responsibility for them.

The author of this book does not dispense medical advice or prescribe the use of any technique as a form of treatment for physical, emotional, or medical problems without the advice of a physician, either directly or indirectly. The intent of the author is only to offer information of a general nature to help you in your quest for emotional and spiritual well-being. In the event you use any of the information in this book for yourself, which is your constitutional right, the author and the publisher assume no responsibility for your actions.

Any people depicted in stock imagery provided by Getty Images are models, and such images are being used for illustrative purposes only. Certain stock imagery © Getty Images.

Print information available on the last page.

ISBN: 978-1-9822-6105-4 (sc)
ISBN: 978-1-9822-6106-1 (e)

Balboa Press rev. date: 02/11/2021

CONTENTS

INTRODUCTION

"So, it has always been about me?" my client whispered as he sat on the couch across from me; slightly shaking his head and rubbing his hands together. "I understand what it means now when you say, I need to find my power. I think I just did."

Throughout my journey working with both teen and adult clients, I began taking note of when they were having their biggest ah-ha moments. I found over and over again, it was when they realized that they held the power to everything; every choice, decision, thought, feeling. Yes, all of it was in their control. I began calling these "Power of Me" moments. These moments produced an understanding of Self, which allowed my clients to live with acceptance, purpose, and joy.

As I continued to use the Power Topics described in this book, clients continued to have amazing revelations, such as,"I realize the only one I am hurting is me, I have the power to change that," "I understand that my anxiety is based on my thoughts. Now I have the power to control that," and "I wish everyone could learn these topics."

Helping my clients discover that their joy was within their power was the most rewarding thing I have ever been part of. When I reveled in their growth, I also sat back to revel in mine, because without my own "power of me" moments, I would not be able to help others find theirs.

I learned that even in dark times, we never truly disconnect from ourselves. We are never truly alone. I learned that each of us has the power to make the changes we need to feel better. We just have to be ready. We have to be willing to find the power within.

Today I have a passion to share my truth, my light, and my love with others so they can find and share theirs. This is the ripple effect that will be passed on to you so you can share your light as well.

This book will give you the strategies needed to help guide you on your path of evolvement. However, evolvement takes commitment. It takes strength to look within in order to uncover wounds that need healing. It takes determination to let go of control and the need for others to love us or be someone different to please us. It takes dedication and discipline to master your mind and live authentically; to believe in your goodness, to love yourself with compassion. Discovering that you are responsible for you, all of you, is when you wake up to your truth. Your happiness is in your control; your thoughts are in your control; your emotions are in your control! I learned this, my clients learned this, and now you can learn it too.

The words that follow are for you take; to turn them into your thoughts and put them into practice in your life.

"Very few people know

who they truly are..."

~~~~~~

THE POWER OF THOUGHT

Thoughts Influence Everything. It is important to understand how powerful your thoughts are. Thoughts are connected to every other Power Topic in this book. You take your thoughts everywhere with you, every second of every day. Your thoughts create everything for you; they create your experiences, perceptions, emotions, feelings and reactions.

Many thoughts you have throughout the day don't actually manifest into a sensation you feel in your body. You can have thousands of thoughts a day and not feel anything about them. Then there are the other thoughts that manifest into an emotion which can be felt within your body. The thoughts that manifest into a physical sensation in your body have a purpose; the feeling is telling you something.

Defining what the feeling actually means is difficult for many. This is due to a lack of understanding surrounding your thoughts and emotional awareness; you have never been given the proper tools to work with this process correctly. You don't know how to break down your reactions, feelings, emotions and thoughts in order to determine how they tie together. However, this book will give you the power to do just that! When you grasp how to think this way, you will be on the path to discovering…your true self.

Here is a diagram and explanation to help you break it down.

The "me" ladder

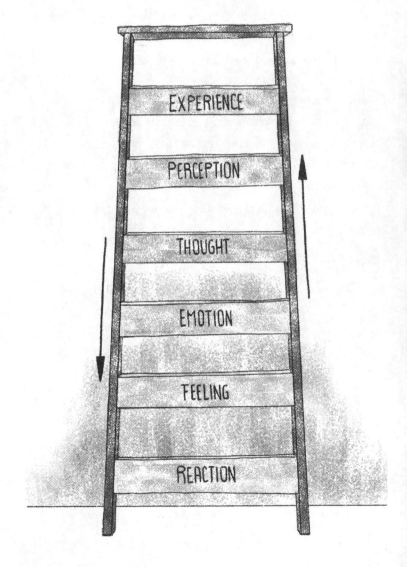

1 - You have an experience. An experience is anything that leaves an impression on you. The impact of this experience will elicit a thought, emotion, feeling and reaction. You can participate willingly, or unwillingly, in any experience that leaves an impression on you.

2 - You form a perception about that experience. Your perception of an experience will be different from everyone around you. Fifty people in the same room having the same experience will all perceive it differently. Someone might pick out something from that experience that resonates with other experiences they have had. Or, they may take something good, or maybe something bad, away from that experience based on the emotions they are currently holding. It is important to note that each person is unique and everyone is at a different place on their journey. Therefore, they will all have their own individual perception of every experience.

3 - You create a thought around the perceived experience. You choose a thought about the perceived experience that fits with your understanding, current beliefs and opinions, that again, are only unique to you.

4 - Your created thought turns into an emotion. The emotion that registers with you is based on the thought you created from the perception of your experience. The emotion will register as either positive or negative.

5 - The emotion then manifests into a feeling. The feeling can then be felt in your physical body. If it is a positive emotion, you feel good and it may be felt in your heart, by chills running throughout your body or you could feel a warm sensation. If it is a negative emotion, you feel bad and it may be felt by a pain in your neck or head, stomach or back.

6 - An individual reaction is chosen based on your feeling.
A reaction is chosen based on the thoughts, emotions and feelings around your experience. Here is where your power lies: How you choose to react to experiences in life is your choice; your reaction is based on your thoughts.

Let's take a look at how this process works using Sadie and Olivia whom are both participating in an orientation that will prepare them to become exchange students.

Experience – Participation in an exchange student orientation seminar.

Sadie

Perception – "That was a lot of information but it will sink in with time. It was a very helpful experience. I was very engaged and learned so much."

Thought – "I am ready for this trip. I have some nerves but that is normal. It will all work out. I am going to learn so much and it will be so fun! I am so blessed."

Emotion – Joy, Excitement, Clarity

Feeling – Relaxed, Ease, Calm, Sleeping well

Reaction – Understanding, Optimism, Self-Aware

Olivia

Perception – "That was way too much information. How will I retain all of this? It was not a helpful experience. I didn't learn anything."

Thought – "I am not ready for this trip. I can't do this. I am way too nervous. I don't know what to expect. How will I even prepare? This is going to be a disaster. I am so dumb."

Emotion – Fear, Anxiety, Confusion

Feeling – Headaches, Stomach pain, Lack of Sleep

Reaction – Lack of Understanding, Pessimism, Unaware

Sadie and Olivia both shared the same experience but both of them perceived it differently. Their individual perception created different emotions, feelings and reactions based on the thoughts they chose.

Sadie chose to look at the experience through the eyes of excitement and self-compassion. She knows she is human so some anxiety is normal. She embraces her feeling of anxiety by acknowledging it. She says, "its ok to feel this way, I will be experiencing something new and different." She gave herself permission to let all the new information digest. Sadie didn't get stuck on a thought that would bring fear and anxiety. She feels it and recognizes it and works with it. She determines what emotions and thoughts are connected to her feelings. She lets herself feel everything because she understands it is normal. In understanding this, she also understands that negative thoughts will not serve her. She lets them pass by focusing on the exciting experience ahead. She gives her time and attention to the thoughts that make her feel good. She doesn't let the thoughts that make her feel bad intensify. She catches them and works with them. Controlled thoughts are like leaves in a nice pile or a ball sitting stationary on top of a hill. They are still there but they have not spiraled out of control. Sadie uses her power and stops the negative thoughts by accepting them and shifting them. She is able to manage them with **disciplined** thinking.

"When you shift your thoughts to something that feels better, you are showing compassion and understanding for yourself."

To shift the above analogy into the opposite, when thoughts become exaggerated, they are like leaves blowing in the wind or a ball rolling quickly down a hill. One negative thought turns into another and before you know it, your thoughts are out of control. Now your negative thoughts have control over you in a damaging way. They have manifested into negative self-talk which will hold you back from experiencing joy and new experiences. This is how Olivia let her thoughts take control of her.

Olivia's thoughts manifested into fear-based thinking. Her thoughts told her that she didn't know enough; her thoughts told her that she was too uncertain of the future. These thoughts escalated and became **undisciplined.** She failed to give herself the time needed to digest the information; she expected she *should* know everything and have it all figured out immediately. She disregarded her need for self-compassion. She did not acknowledge the emotions she was feeling by saying, "I feel you anxiety but I've got this. I don't need you to stop me from looking forward to a great experience. I will figure it out as I go." She let her emotions become her. She became anxiety. She became fear. She became doubt.

What Olivia failed to recognize is that she is not her thoughts or emotions. Rather her thoughts, emotions and feelings are just indicators. They help us make decisions and direct our life onto the right path. Remember, you control what and how you think.

Olivia's thoughts needed shifting. She got stuck on her negative thoughts. The more she got stuck there, the more her thoughts escalated. As her thoughts escalated, more negative emotion was generated, thus, causing her reactions to be negative. It is much harder to rake leaves into a pile when they are scattered for miles. That is exactly what happened to Olivia's thoughts. She let them scatter instead of embracing them and shifting them to thoughts that felt better.

You are not your mind. You are not your thoughts. You are not your feelings. You are not your emotions. You are you. **And YOU are SO much more.**

Understanding the "me ladder" allows you to work with the sensations in your body. Knowing that each feeling is connected back to a thought gives you permission to work with the related thought. To reiterate, when you have a feeling in your physical body it is connected to an emotion; the emotion is connected to a thought; and the thought is connected to your perception of a past or present experience.

> **"It is the way you look at experiences that create the struggle. The struggle is always within yourself. It takes a conscious effort to look at experiences in your life from the right perspective. The ability to do this will elicit thoughts and emotions that align with your true self. When you find the place of alignment, you will feel joy, each and every time."**

Beliefs

Negative thoughts that you think about over and over again aren't going to feel better if you think about them longer. This is known as *overthinking.* Thinking discouraging thoughts repeatedly only exaggerates them until they eventually define your future thinking. This is how self-limiting beliefs are created.

A self-limiting belief is a negative thought you have thought for so long that it now holds power over you. These beliefs hold you back; such as, "I am so dumb." "I am not good enough." "I am not worthy." "Life is scary and hard." "Nothing ever works out." "Bad things always happen to me." "I have nothing to offer." "I am not beautiful."

These self-limiting beliefs turn into patterns of behavior that keep you from experiencing your full potential, your true joy and your true self. You begin avoiding things in life that could bring you enjoyment and excitement based on these false beliefs. You become scared to embrace future endeavors; you worry about what other people think of you; you face situations with struggle and a bad attitude.

What is so amazing about thinking is, every thought can feel good. Which means, every negative thought can always be shifted to something that feels better!

What thought feels better to you?

I am dumb.	I am intelligent.
I don't deserve this.	I am worthy.
I can't do this.	I am strong and capable.
Life is so hard.	Life is rewarding.
I have nothing to offer.	I have a special gift to share.
I am not attractive.	I am beautiful.

Now you are beginning to see how your thoughts create your experiences.

Self-limiting beliefs will hold you back from having positive experiences because experiences will always match your perception of yourself.

So, if thoughts influence experiences, then the same belief system must hold true for positive thoughts. If you think positive thoughts over and over again, they will also become beliefs. Yet these beliefs are not limiting. These beliefs are uplifting and encouraging. They instill confidence and security. These thoughts are based on self-compassion and personal empowerment. Ultimately, thinking positive thoughts that feel good will align you to your true self and give you a sense of purpose in life. These thoughts will create positive experiences in your life because, again, experiences match your perception of yourself.

Life is supposed to feel joyful to you; life is supposed to be fun. If it doesn't feel this way, you are not aligned with your true self. When life doesn't feel good, your feelings, thus your emotions, thus your thoughts, thus your perceptions are not aligned with your true self.

I often have clients tell me, "this is all very logical but disciplining your thoughts is extremely hard to do." I respond by saying, "Yes, you are right. It is hard to do." It takes time, self-control and awareness in order to take back your power of thought; but once you do it a few times, it gets easier. Each time you acknowledge and stop a thought before it escalates, you are experiencing a *"power of me"* moment. Keeping your power allows you to control your thinking. Controlling your thoughts allows you to shift them when necessary to thoughts that feel better. When your thoughts have created an unsatisfactory feeling, just remember these words: Acknowledge, understand, accept and then shift.

You can see here how powerful you become when you shift your thoughts. What feels better to you, reading the misaligned thoughts or the controlled thoughts? The controlled thoughts give you the feeling of empowerment. The feeling of confidence and acceptance means you are aligned with your true self.

Start paying attention to how often you have "what if", "I can't" or "I should" thoughts. These thoughts are holding you back from having a "power of me" moment. They create fear and judgment and they don't accept you where you are right now in your life. They steal away the joy and excitement from new experiences.

Below is an example of misaligned thinking versus aligned thinking when starting a new job.

Misaligned Scattered Thoughts
I am so overwhelmed. What if nobody likes me? What if
I don't like my boss? What if I make a mistake? I don't
have enough to offer. I am going to look like a mess. I
will probably screw this up. People are going to stare
at me. I am sure they will think I am an ugly disaster.

Aligned Controlled Thoughts
It is the first day. First days of anything always bring a
sense of anticipation and nerves. This is normal. I am ok. I
am prepared. Everything always works out for me. I know
how to do this job. I already met the boss and he liked me.
I am excited to meet new people. I am strong and brave.

Visualize this:
Your mind is the car. Your thoughts are
the driver. How do you want to be driven
in life? Weaving and scattering all over
the road or between the lines?

You have the power to decide!

POWER OF THOUGHT
EXERCISES

1. Fill in the blank template below for a thought you carry that is misaligned. Then shift it to a thought that feels better, that aligns with your truth. Fill in the other side.

Misaligned Scattered Thought	Aligned Scattered Thought
_____	_____
_____	_____
_____	_____
_____	_____
_____	_____
_____	_____
_____	_____
_____	_____
_____	_____
_____	_____
_____	_____

Misaligned Scattered Thought

Aligned Scattered Thought

_____ _____

_____ _____

_____ _____

_____ _____

_____ _____

_____ _____

_____ _____

_____ _____

_____ _____

_____ _____

_____ _____

_____ _____

_____ _____

_____ _____

_____ _____

_____ _____

_____ _____

2. Using the me ladder, write about a negative experience you had and follow it down the ladder writing about your perception, thought, emotion, feeling and reaction. Then work yourself back up the ladder, starting at the bottom by choosing a different reaction. Go all the way back up changing each rung into a positive.

_____

_____

_____

_____

_____

_____

_____

_____

_____

_____

_____

_____

_____

_____

_____

_____

_____

_____

_____

3. Write the words *Acknowledge, Understand and Accept.* Then describe an experience that created negative thoughts. Write about how you can accept this experience. Create a new perception by choosing thoughts that are more positive.

_____

_____

_____

_____

_____

_____

_____

_____

_____

_____

_____

_____

_____

_____

_____

_____

_____

_____

_____

_____

_____

~~~~~~

THE POWER OF EMOTION

Most emotions have a label of either positive or negative. However, using the word "negative" to associate with emotion has led our society to believe that anytime one feels a negative emotion that they are "bad" for feeling it. A false belief is instilled that our emotions define us.

Beginning in childhood, we may hear that we should not feel a certain way, that we need to stop crying and be strong. This often leads to feeling shame because we don't want to let others down by feeling a certain way.

Young boys are often told that if they are sensitive or show and feel emotion, that they are weak. Therefore, they often grow up confused about emotions and either push them away or react in attacking ways. We may think something is wrong with us when we have intense emotion and we don't know what to do when they surface. Thus, we end up stowing them away and not acknowledging them; having a false belief that it is unsafe to feel.

Due to living in a culture that has not typically supported emotional awareness, you have grown up without the proper tools. You are not taught that negative emotions are healthy. You were never taught that emotions are actually teaching you about yourself; your true self.

It is paramount to understand that all emotions are essential. You need to feel negative emotions in order to know what positive emotions are. Knowing what feels bad allows you to make the necessary changes so you can feel good. You were born with both sets of emotions for a reason. When you comprehend this, you will begin recognizing that they are your own teacher. Emotions are your indicators; they navigate you through life; they are your own personal compass. Having knowledge about what your emotions are telling you creates personal empowerment.

When you appreciate that emotions are a tool to help you navigate through life, you will be more compassionate and accepting in allowing them to surface. It is like a little kid tugging on your arm to get your attention. You aren't going to turn to them and yell, "Stop being annoying!" You would instead acknowledge them. You would give them the respect and compassion they deserve as you determine what it is that they want and need.

This is exactly what your emotions want when you can feel them. They are tugging at you to listen. They want you to acknowledge them and become aware of what they are telling you. You are feeling them for a reason. So, when you have a feeling, stop and acknowledge it. Where do you feel it in your body? Determine what emotion created the feeling and what thought created the emotion. Is it positive or negative? Then determine what you have learned from this emotion. Is it an emotion you want to recreate or is it connected to thoughts that need to be shifted? Did a desire manifest or is there something still unfulfilled? Is there work to be done to learn or did you embrace a new understanding?

"All emotions are important. They are not to be disregarded or ignored. When they don't feel good, they are offering you important information. You have the power to learn from your emotions. What are they teaching you?"

Using your emotions as a tool is vital as you continue to expand and change in life. What is important to note is, you will constantly be fluctuating between all sorts of emotions, negative and positive and emotions in-between. This is normal and this is healthy. It becomes unhealthy when you get stuck on negative thoughts that create negative emotions; this means that you are unable to climb up and down the "me ladder" freely between experiences, thoughts, feelings and emotions. Getting stuck on a thought that creates a negative emotion will never bring you joy.

"The Trail of Emotions" is an easy analogy to help define emotions. Remember, all emotions are valuable and healthy and all emotions stem from your thoughts. You need the negative ones just as much as the positive ones. The only difference is you don't want to "camp out" on the negative side. It is not a good place to stay for long.

On the negative trail, it is rocky and there could be quicksand. When you are walking on the negative trails, it is time to be alert and aware to how you feel. On these trails you might notice that you tire fast; you may begin to feel exhausted as a lot of your energy is being spent. However, even though you may feel stress walking this trail, it is an important time for you to learn something. This trail is offering you an opportunity for introspection. The lessons you learn on the negative trails are what you put into action when you are back on the positive trails. The realizations you learn will also help you appreciate the positive trails even more.

On the positive trail you feel at ease. It is where you want to stay longer; it is where you revel in your experiences. Feeling the positive emotion on this trail allows you to know you are on the right track. You don't need to rush or feel stressed. You notice the clear beauty. It is on the positive trail where you have time to relax and feel joy by loving, accepting, appreciating and anticipating. When you feel good you know you are aligned with your true self, your truth.

How do you become stuck with negative emotion?

Blame

When you were young it was often hard to talk about your emotions because you didn't have the proper vocabulary. As a child you were not taught what emotions truly mean, so you got very good at repressing and blaming. You didn't understand that your thoughts create emotion and that is why you feel. This lack of understanding, as you got older, caused you to look outside of yourself for blame. You wanted someone to fix how you felt because you had no idea that you had the power to do this yourself. So, you set out to defend your position and blame others for making you feel a certain way. "It is all their fault; I can't believe they did that to me; they hurt my feelings; they are so mean; are they ever going to change?" Sound familiar? You said those things because you didn't understand that no one can *truly* hurt your feelings. No one needs to change for you. Your feelings are the result of your thoughts. Giving your power away and asking others to change their behavior to make you feel better will never work.

"Using your emotions as a tool is vital as you continue to expand and change in life. What is important to note is, you will constantly be fluctuating between all sorts of emotions, negative and positive and emotions in-between. This is normal and this is healthy."

There are a lot of people in your life, strangers and loved ones, and it's quite certain that they are not *all* going to be perfect for you. When you ask them to do things different so you feel better, you are giving them your power. As well, asking them to be different isn't accepting them for where they are on their journey in life. They are having their own experiences that are helping shape them into who they are, just as you are. So, asking them to change means you want someone else to have the power to change your thoughts and emotions. This is backwards and it is exhausting. Learning that it is much easier for you to keep your own power and change your own thoughts is exhilarating. It lets everyone off the hook and it helps you learn empowerment. You learn that you can feel good all the time, regardless of what anyone else is doing and you can accept others for who they are and where they are on their journey. Keeping your power breeds understanding, acceptance and compassion for yourself and for others.

Ignoring the Emotion

When you don't recognize your negative emotions, you are actually ignoring your own indicator for personal growth and healing. The pain and hurt is an indication that you have given your power away; you are not climbing back up the ladder to see how the pain and hurt manifested. Instead you remain stuck at the bottom waiting for a rope to fall even though you have a ladder to climb. When you wait for the rope to fall you stay stuck at the bottom, only able to look at things the same way. It keeps you feeling trapped and unempowered. Instead, when you climb the ladder, you begin to see things from a different view, from a new perspective. You become empowered when you see things with clarity; with an understanding that every feeling and thought is within your control.

Ignoring negative sensations in your body means you fail to understand the process. All you know is you don't feel good. When you realize that YOU are the reason you don't feel good is when you begin to take back your power. When you stop waiting for the rope to drop and you start climbing up the ladder in front of you, you are having a power of me moment.

You need to understand that emotions don't want to be repressed! They want to be acknowledged, heard, and listened to! Remember the little kid tugging on your arm? When you don't acknowledge your emotions with compassion, they come out in unhealthy ways.

When you have outbursts of frustration, anger or rage, turn to food, bodily harm, alcohol, prescription and/or illegal drugs, or other types of addictions, you are expressing emotions in a negative way. Sometimes you may want to run away, move away, or just get out of town. You have a mindset that coping in these ways will dissolve the bad feelings; that the emotion will just disappear.

As you learn to recognize all emotions, you become powerful. Having the ability to shift thoughts associated with negative emotion and recreate thoughts that elicit positive emotion allows you to live a life of understanding and purpose.

The reason you turn to these methods in order to cope is because you have never been taught emotional awareness. All you know is that you want relief so you partake in adverse behavior in hopes it will make you feel better. However, this will never bring about permanent reprieve. The relief that is felt is only temporary because you are not fixing or dealing with the root cause. No amount of negative coping will ever fix the real reason you don't feel good. Your perception around your experience and the thought tied to the emotion are all still there, hidden away, waiting for you to feel them another day.

Here is what happens. The thoughts will arise again. Then they become an emotion that doesn't feel good and you will do the only thing you know how to do, seek temporary relief. This is how you create unhealthy patterns. This cycle of coping continues to harbor the negative emotion in your body. When it gets ignored, it returns to a resting place within you. Each time it returns, it begins to manifest; the cells in your body are now transforming into something more; repressed emotions will eventually turn into stress and physical and mental illness.

Remember, you take yourself everywhere. This means that your thoughts and emotions go everywhere with you too. You can't get stuck at the bottom of the ladder or on the negative trail. The only thing that will make you feel better is building emotional strength. You need to climb back up the ladder and leave the grips of the negative trail.

When you climb the ladder, you acknowledge; and when you walk the trails, you feel. This can be painful in the beginning, especially when you are climbing the ladder or escaping the grips of the negative trail for the first time. Anything you do for the first time is difficult. Just like physical exercise is difficult when you first begin, so is building your emotional strength. However, each time you climb (the ladder) and each time you break free (of the negative trail), you get stronger. As you build stamina, you begin to see that you have the biggest influence over your life. When you become aware of this, your motivation to become aligned with your true self intensifies because of how good you feel. Recognizing that your strength comes from within you, and not outside of you, is finding your power.

"You can't get stuck at the bottom of the ladder or on the negative trail. The only thing that will make you feel better is building emotional strength. You need to climb back up the ladder and leave the grips of the negative trail."

Let's Review

Now is the time to take back your power of emotion. You do this by understanding that you are not bad or wrong for having a negative emotion, you are human. Your emotions don't define you. They guide you. Your emotions are yours. They are based on your thoughts. You are the only one that has the power to change what you think. No one outside of you has that power. As well, it is not the job of others to make sure you feel good. It is your job to make sure you feel good and it is their job to make themselves feel good. If you are always giving your power to someone else and asking them to be different so you can feel better, you will never experience true joy.

As you learn to listen to your body and how you feel, you will begin to tune into the thoughts that ignited your emotions. When you have an experience that elicits a negative emotion, you won't want to get stuck there. You will have the strength to acknowledge and work yourself backwards to figure out which thoughts fueled the feeling. As you determine which thought brought forth the negative emotion, you can recognize the emotion and shift the thought to something that feels better. They more you do this, the easier it gets and the more joyful moments you will have. When you have a joyful experience, it will be felt and you will want to recreate more experiences that elicit the same feeling. As you climb up and down the ladder and navigate the emotional trails you will no longer feel stuck; you will feel like you have been set free.

Having a relationship with your emotions shows strength; acknowledging your emotions shows courage; knowing you have a right to your emotions shows acceptance. This is a power of me moment.

POWER OF EMOTION
EXERCISES

1. Write about a time in your life when you waited for the rope to fall. Were you placing blame on someone else for your life experience? How did you feel? Now start thinking about climbing up the ladder, looking at this experience in a new perspective, from within you, not outside of you. How does it change the way you feel?

_____

_____

_____

_____

_____

_____

_____

_____

_____

_____

_____

_____

_____

_____

_____

2. Using the trail of emotions as a guide, journal about a negative thought that kept you stuck feeling a negative emotion. Take that emotion and work yourself out of the negative trail, choosing a different thought along the way that brings you to a new emotion. You might need to make a few stops on the way before you are back to the positive side. Just keep moving. Don't get stuck.

_____

_____

_____

_____

_____

_____

_____

_____

_____

_____

_____

_____

_____

_____

_____

_____

_____

_____

_____

_____

THE POWER OF NOW

The past is your log book of everything you have created and everything you have experienced. It is your storehouse of fruitful memories and painful moments. All of them shaping and molding you into who you are today.

It is the beautiful ones you joyfully daydream about and hold close to your heart. As you flip through the pages of your book, these memories bring about a positive feeling. You spend time trying to recreate more moments that will elicit this same sensation. They are the experiences that you want to add to your book in permanent ink.

Then there are also the painful moments. The ones you wish you could erase from your book. The ones you wish didn't exist. The painful ones that hurt so bad. They are the ones that bring out the negative thoughts, emotions and reactions. They elicit anger and rage; they bring you to your knees in sadness; they make your head spin in frustration, disbelief and disappointment.

Even though you wish you would have used a pencil so you could erase some of those moments, ironically, they are also the ones that can get etched so deep. Why? Because you dwell on them over and over. And, as you dwell on them, it is like writing on top of the same words over and over until the page rips. Then when the page rips, you get upset and feel bad about your book being tattered. You are mad at yourself or you want to seek revenge on someone else. You fill your head with negative thoughts about yourself or you try hold someone else accountable for ripping the pages of your book.

OLD ME

SAD AND REGRET FOR THE PAST

FEAR AND WORRY FOR FUTURE

FOCUSED ON PAST AND/OR FUTURE: NOT LIVING IN THE PRESENT

However, what you need to remember is, YOU are the one that actually ripped your own book. You got stuck there. You held onto the negative thoughts based on your perception of your experience. You are the only one thinking those thoughts. You are the only one holding onto those emotions. You are the one talking bad to yourself. No one else is, only you. There will never be another person who can control your perception, thoughts or emotions. That ability is within your power and your power only. You are unique; and as you live life, you are writing your own book. You have the choice to give gratitude and forgiveness to yourself and others or you can choose not to. You can accept your experiences with gratitude and understanding or you can get stuck replaying them and living them over and over. You have the power.

> "There will never be another person who can control your perception, thoughts or emotions. That ability is within your power and your power only."

Knowing you are human is the first step in understanding your past. As a human being living on this planet, you have had a lot of experiences. Every day you change and expand into something more based on your experiences and your emotions. Your life story would be incomplete if it was only filled with the good. It wouldn't be a representation of real life and it would not be a practical way to help you learn and grow. Understanding that your story needs the negative parts to make the good parts even better is key.

After you have had a negative experience, it is important to give yourself time to feel; to reflect while you climb back up the ladder. When you get back up to the thoughts that were created from that experience, you can shift them. It is knowing that you can take something good out of each moment even if it brought you to your knees; even if it created trauma. Because there are no mistakes in life, only lessons. It is learning how to look for the lesson and let the pain go that will bring about healing.

I have had clients ask how they can possibly give gratitude for past experiences that have brought them hurt and pain. Each time, I give the same response, "Because without that experience, you would not be the person sitting in front of me. Every experience has helped shape you into you. And the "you" that is sitting in front of me right now is amazing."

You can think of any experience and take something good away from it. You are growing and changing and every experience offers you an opportunity to expand. You get to decide how you want to react to your experiences. You have that power. If you are having a hard time understanding how this is even possible, here are some examples:

Negative Past Experience	Positive Outcome
I got fired from my job.	That job taught me a lot of things I like but also a lot of things I did not like. As I start applying for new jobs, I will now know which ones resonate with me.
I was raped.	Because of this experience, I found my worth and empowerment. I have learned the true meaning of forgiveness. I ended up getting a degree in social work. I am also a volunteer in a women's shelter. I am passionate about what I do every day. I am making a difference. I am courageous.

My partner left me.	Even though this hurt, I have recognized many things that were not healthy in our relationship. I have spent a lot of time getting to know myself and building the confidence and security I never had. This experience has helped me recognize and deal with a lot of things I always ignored. I feel lighter and happier.
My parents abused me or abandoned me.	I have learned how to deal with triggers in a healthy way. I have grown to be independent; knowing I am safe and secure on my own. I am comfortable in my own skin. I am a better parent because of what I experienced. I can recognize that I am a better person today for my past experiences. I am grateful.
I was arrested for possession of drugs.	Getting caught was the best thing that ever happened to me. I want a healthy future. I want to treat my body with respect and care. I want to learn the right way to deal with my feelings that led me to substance abuse in the first place. I no longer want to give my power and control away to a drug. I am worth it. I have learned how amazing it feels to keep my power!

> **"There will never be another person who can control your perception, thoughts or emotions. That ability is within your power and your power only."**

Don't live in the past. In many cases, *living in the past leads to depressive thoughts.* Accepting your past and being aware that everything worked out exactly as intended, gives you a sense of appreciation.

Don't get stuck on the negative; dwelling, resenting and expecting someone else to fix things. It is not their job. It is your job to understand how you need to learn and grow from each experience. Take some time to process each event in your life, but know, no matter what, that you are ok. Every experience helped create you! You don't need anyone to change. You don't need any experience to be different. Give gratitude for the past and let the rest go. Live in the now!

Look in the mirror and see the person you are today. Embrace and love that person right now. Talk to yourself with compassion. You are unique and special and you are on your own personal journey. Write in your book with conviction that your past has created the person you see today and the person you see is strong and brave. That is a power of me moment.

The Future

Thoughts that elicit an emotion of worry translate into a fear of the future. Future based thinking that leads to worry is fear-based thinking. These are the "what-if" statements you say to yourself over and over again. They are the questions you ask yourself that you don't have the answers for so you spend time trying to fill in the blanks.

Living in the future means you don't trust the process of life; it means you want to have it all planned out. So, you spend your time doing, stressing and preparing. This type of fear-based thinking, or over-thinking, uses up valuable energy and steals the joy away from your present moment experiences.

Living in the future can cause feelings of anxiety. Anxiety and worry are negative thoughts associated with the future. When you get stuck on those thoughts, you never truly enjoy life.

I have had clients tell me, "But I need to be prepared for the worst because then I won't be let down when bad things happen." This is a very common, and normal, thought process when you don't understand emotional awareness and personal empowerment.

> **"When you accept the lessons you are here to learn, you continue to evolve into the best version of YOU."**

Let's Evaluate This Way of Thinking.
First, it is important to recognize that preparing for some things in life is practical but it needs to be done with the right thought process. There is a difference between preparing with acceptance, optimism, anticipation and excitement and preparing with fear, pessimism, worry and a lack of trust. Choosing thoughts about the future that create images of things you don't want creates fear.

Choosing thoughts about the future that create images of things you do want, creates excitement. It makes life fun and rewarding. It is like being on a daily quest and each new experience is an opportunity for more treasure.

> **"Worry is creating an image in your mind of everything you do not want to happen. Anticipation is creating an image in your mind of everything you do want to happen. What images do you want to create?**

Second, you can't prepare for everything, nor would you want to. What fun would life actually be if you could? It would strip the anticipation out of each new experience. You would never know the feeling of surprise and the emotion of desire. Your story would be boring to read. It would be perfectly planned out and orchestrated exactly as you want so you never have to feel negative emotion. This is not real life and it is not why we are here on this journey. This journey is intended for growth; an ever-changing expansion into more. If you never have any negative experiences and emotions to learn and grow from, you would never evolve.

As well, remember that what you "think" you are preparing for, never works out as you planned anyway. It is life's way of letting you know the true reason why you are here. It is not to control the process; it is to participate in the process.

So, stop trying to have it all planned out. It is exhausting. Trust the process of life and what you are here to learn. Let it play out, one day at a time, as it is meant to be, and enjoy right now.

The Present

There is only now. Now is all there is and all there ever will be. Now is where you live and breathe. The past cannot be changed and the future cannot be predicted. If your thoughts are always on the past or on the future, you are not living in the present. Life is passing you by and the joy of your present experiences are never truly being felt. Now is also where you have the power to control what you think about. When you live in the present, you are giving yourself ample opportunities to have power of me moments by shifting your thoughts. Each time you shift your thoughts to something that feels better you are moving closer to experiencing joy!

NEW ME

APPRECIATION FOR PAST

SATISFACTION FOR PRESENT

EXCITEMENT FOR FUTURE

The past is what you accept and where you give gratitude.

The future is what you anticipate with excitement.

The present is where you experience joy!

"Whether you have experienced something negative or positive, every moment is offering you something to be grateful for. What are you being presented with right now that you can appreciate?"

POWER OF NOW EXERCISES

1. Present: Make a list of all the things you appreciate in your life today. What do you have to be grateful for right now?

Past: Knowing that something positive can be taken from everything that happens in your life, knowing that nothing went wrong, that everything happens for your own personal evolution, how can you change how you look at past experiences in your life?

Future: Set some intentions for the future. What do you want to manifest? Make a list or a collage of all the things you dream of. Live with a grateful heart, give appreciation for your past and present and look to your future with anticipation; knowing that everything you want, and believe you can have, is on its way.

_____

_____

_____

_____

_____

_____

_____

_____

_____

_____

_____

_____

2. Using the t-chart, choose a past experience that you have deemed negative. Then, determine what positive outcome you learned from that experience.

Negative Past Experience   **Positive Outcome**

_____   _____

_____   _____

_____   _____

_____   _____

_____   _____

_____   _____

_____   _____

_____   _____

_____   _____

_____   _____

_____   _____

_____   _____

_____   _____

Negative Past Experience   **Positive Outcome**

_____   _____

_____   _____

_____   _____

_____   _____

_____   _____

_____   _____

_____   _____

_____   _____

_____   _____

_____   _____

_____   _____

_____   _____

_____   _____

*Remember, all past hurt and heartache can
be released. It does not serve you anymore
and holding onto the hurt is only holding you
back. You cannot change the past, you can only
accept it. Take the lesson and let the rest go.*

THE POWER OF AWARENESS

Being aware means, you have the ability to recognize feelings in your body and decipher what they mean. It is tuning into the sensations that arise and determining what emotions they are tied to. It is acknowledging the emotions and clarifying the thoughts you have been thinking.

As a child you were raised to listen. Right? Listen to your parents, listen to your teachers, listen to your coaches. You were instructed to listen to everyone outside of you. But, were you ever taught to listen to yourself?

Obviously, it is important to learn how to listen to your parents and the adults in your life. Their guidance and wisdom can be crucial in helping you along your journey. However, there are times when you might already know your own answers or want to listen to your own inner guide because you just have a feeling. Yet, you were persuaded in another direction by someone outside of you, left to ignore your own inner wisdom.

Continually pleasing others while ignoring your own guide will lead to unhealthy patterns of "people pleasing." This pattern of behavior causes you to lose connection to your true self because you focus on making sure others feel good and not yourself. Over time it becomes very difficult to listen and trust your own guidance. You have a hard time tuning into your own indicators because, in order to hear what others are saying, you had to tune yourself out.

It is not traditionally understood by our culture that emotional awareness and listening to physical feelings is valuable. There is a failure in our society to understand the impact this has on health and overall joy. You are not taught how to listen to your body; there is no education around acceptance of emotions and using them as a guide. Having awareness and tuning into your emotions is a very important tool in owning your power and embracing your individuality.

"It is not traditionally understood by our culture that emotional awareness and listening to physical feelings is valuable. There is a failure in our society to understand the impact this has on health and overall joy. You are not taught how to listen to your body; there is no education around acceptance of emotions and using them as a guide."

Once you can become aware of your thoughts and emotions, your connection to yourself will become strong. You will discover that answers to your questions are already within you. You don't have to listen to anyone else. With this awareness, you can relax and build an amazing relationship with your deepest friend, You! It is true that no one knows you better than you. Being aware means being connected; being connected helps you uncover your truth.

In order to connect with yourself, you have to know yourself. In order to know yourself, you have to give yourself ample opportunities to experience joy. Spending more time doing the things you enjoy, aligns you with your true self.

Have you ever heard anyone say, "I need some alone time?" or "I need to clear my head?" This is essentially what they are trying to do. They are trying to connect to their true self. They don't actually know they are doing this, but they are. They are seeking clarity. When you participate in activities that bring you to a sense of calm, a sense of peace, you become connected. By quieting the mind through meditation, quiet walks in nature, or doing anything else you love to do in solitude, you are giving yourself the opportunity to connect.

As you continue to find time for these experiences you will begin to feel a greater sense of connection. The more connected you are, the more you are learning about your true self. Through the discovery of yourself, you become aware of your needs and what brings you joy. After time, you will begin recreating more experiences that align with you because you will finally be saying, "now this is me!"

"In order to connect to yourself, you have to know yourself. In order to know yourself you have to give yourself ample opportunities to experience joy."

When you spend time in solitude, you won't need to search for answers or force outcomes. When you are in a place of joyful, peaceful alignment, no work is needed. Answers come from the ease of allowing. The ease of allowing is knowing; the ease of knowing is the power of awareness.

Finding Your Joy

Create a list of all the things you love to do, things you enjoy and things that bring positive sensations. This can be as small as taking a walk, smelling fresh cut lawn, taking a bath, to bigger activities such as, volunteering, taking an arts class or exercising. Look at the list and circle the activities you do often. You may realize that you partake in these activities seldomly. Decide which activities you would like to do more and circle those. These are your "circles of joy."

Sit with the list and look over the circled items, tune into the sensation in your body when you think of doing these things; pay attention to how you feel. Using visualization, brainstorm a list of words or short phrases that quantifies how you feel.

Next, participate in the activity. Document the experience and the reaction associated with it. What sensations did you feel in your body? What emotion did this activity elicit for you?

Joyful experiences are guidance for you. Things that feel good align with your truth. Things that do not feel good do not align with your truth. If it feels good, it is something that your inner being believes in. Joyful feelings are the way your true self tells you that you are on the right path; it says, "more of that please."

Eventually it will become easier to recreate joyful experiences because you will be aware of your feelings, emotions and thoughts. When you recognize more of the things you like, the things you don't like will become clearer as well. Negative experiences, thoughts and emotions will not be tolerated as often. You will understand quicker if you are aligned with the truth of who you are. If you are not, you can use this awareness to shift feelings, emotions, thoughts and experiences to get you back to the positive sensations you have grown to love.

As you continue working with the power of awareness, you are learning how to align with your true self. When you are in alignment, you can feel it. You are holding your power and coming from an enlightened place. These are the moments you want to recreate. When you are feeling sensations of appreciation and reveling in the things that bring you joy, you are connected to your true self.

"Awareness is listening. Being unaware is ignoring."

Awareness in Relationships

One of the greatest benefits of building a relationship with yourself is, every other relationship in your life will benefit. If you want healthy relationships with others, you first have to have a healthy relationship with you. If you don't know who you are and what brings you joy, how do you expect anyone else to add to your joy? As well, if you are asking others to bring you joy because you can't find it on your own, you are putting your power outside of yourself. You are asking others to fill your voids because you cannot fill them yourself. That is asking a lot of someone and there is a high probability that they are going to let you down. You will keep feeling empty and worse yet, your thoughts will be ones that breed resentment and frustration. Not a good place to be.

So instead, when you find your joy first and then seek relationships to add to your joy, you have it mastered. That way when relationships end or change, you know you are still ok. You still have you and you still have your joy. You will see that every relationship complements your life, and as they come and go, you learn and grow. It is the ebb and flow of life. Relationships are meant to teach you about yourself. It is always about you. So, when you build a healthy foundation with Self, you are keeping your power and fostering your awareness. You are able to welcome joyous relationships into your life that will complement the one you share with yourself.

*"When you are in alignment, you can feel it.
These are the moments you want to recreate.
When you are feeling sensations of appreciation
and reveling in the things that bring you
joy, you are connected to your true self."*

POWER OF AWARENESS
EXERCISES

Circles of Joy

1. Make a list of all the things that bring you joy. Circle 5 activities that you will give yourself permission to do more. After you partake in your joyful activity, answer these questions.

- What was your joyful experience?
- What sensation did you feel in your body as you were having this experience?
- Where did you feel it in your body?
- What emotion was this feeling tied to?
- What thoughts do you have about this experience?
- How does this activity help you know you are in alignment with your true self?

_____

_____

_____

_____

_____

_____

_____

_____

_____

_____

_____

_____

2. All of our relationships in life bring about personal awareness. If someone triggers us, it means that there is still something within us that needs to be healed? Think about relationships in your life that have brought up negative emotion. It isn't about the other person; it is about you. How can you use your relationships as a mirror? What have they triggered in you that requires reflection for your own growth and healing?

_____

_____

_____

_____

_____

_____

_____

_____

_____

_____

_____

_____

_____

_____

_____

_____

_____

_____

_____

_____

_____

_____

_____

_____

_____

_____

_____

_____

_____

_____

_____

_____

_____

_____

_____

_____

_____

_____

_____

_____

3. Get out in nature, meditate and do breathing exercises to quiet your mind, find the answers you seek and align your thoughts to present moment joys.

THE POWER OF CONTROL

The only thing you will ever control in life is yourself. You will never be able to control another person's thoughts, behaviors or reactions. You cannot. What you can control is you, right now, in this present moment. You have the power to control your own *thoughts, behaviors and reactions.*

When you try to control, you are doing it from a place of fear. It means you have expectations about how things need to turn out in order for you to feel safe. The emotion of fear stems from the false impression that if things don't turn out the way you want them to be, that if things don't happen the way you plan, you will feel negative emotion. So, you try to control people and situations to keep you from feeling an uncomfortable emotion. What you fail to realize is, the only thing you can control is you. Which means, you have the power to control how you feel. No one outside of you can control how you feel. You have the power to feel safe and secure depending on the thoughts you choose to think. It is remembering that you are in control because the power lies within you, not outside of you.

The need to control situations outside of yourself, gives you a false sense of power by manipulating people and situations, to your liking, in order to feel better. It is like molding clay just the way you want it to be and then telling all the people around you that they need to mold their clay exactly the same as yours. Yet, as you look around, you notice that their clay looks different than yours. Each piece is unique; special to them because they molded it (it is based on their perceptions, thoughts, emotions, all of which you are not able to control). So, you jump up and you run around, trying to make their piece look exactly like yours. However, what you find is, it is impossible to do. No two pieces can ever be molded exactly the same even if you are the one trying. You spend all your time trying to mold situations and people to your liking to find out that you will never have that power. It is no wonder you are exhausted. You have power struggles with others because, as they try to mold their own clay, you want to change it. You don't trust that each piece will turn out exactly as it needs to be.

Taking the clay analogy and putting into real life goes like this: When you ask someone to be different, you are giving away your power. The same thing happens when you try to control a situation. You are giving your power away by believing that your feelings of safety, security and joy depend on how someone else acts and how a situation plays out. Both of these scenarios are ones which you will never have control over. It is realizing that you have the power to choose your thoughts; you have the power to choose how you relate and react to others. Finding your joy is an internal job. It does not come from controlling anything externally.

"Our life is like molding clay. It reflects our personal evolvement throughout life and will look different from all others around us. As we learn how to accept and create our own life with this understanding, we lovingly allow others to create theirs."

First, remember, it is never anyone's job to make you feel joyful. It is their job to find their joy and it's your job to find your joy. You get to keep your power when you choose thoughts and behaviors that align with your true self and when you react to others from a place of love, acceptance and understanding. It is knowing that you don't need anyone to act different or be different for you to feel good because your emotions are in your control. You keep your power when you can accept others for who they are and where they are on their journey without wanting to control or change them.

Second, remember, it is impossible to control future situations. You will never have it all planned out and when you try, it is exhausting and a waste of time and energy. Most important, it takes the thrill out of life. When you trust that things are working out for you and everything will evolve as it is intended, you keep your power and your energy and you give up your need to control.

You can choose how you react to every situation, person, or experience. You get to decide everything you think. How you choose to think, controls how you feel, and how you feel effects your behaviors and your reactions to others.

When you are aligned, you are being true to you and your reaction will be one of understanding and acceptance. If you are not in alignment with your true self, your reaction will be one of anger and hostility. It is important to deal with situations and people from a good place. Positivity breeds more positivity, love and tolerance. Negativity breeds more negativity, hurt and struggle. When you react to others from a place of anger, resentment and defensiveness it only hurts you.

You are the one holding onto the feelings of lack and pain, which only brings you further down.

> **"When you ask someone to be different, you are giving away your power. The same thing happens when you try to control a situation. You are giving your power away by believing that your feelings of safety, security and joy depend on how someone else acts and how a situation plays out."**

The Need to Be Right

Often the need to be right gets in the way of having a positive reaction. What happens is you look to defend your position, trying to force others to have the same thoughts as you. Sometimes you fear judgment and disapproval so you force your opinion onto others and defend your actions through arguments and silent treatments. If you always have a need to be right, it will continuously impact how you relate to others and your relationships will suffer.

As well, most people do not like to take the time for personal reflection. Instead, they look outside of themselves to cast blame. They have a false understanding that proving someone wrong will bring them the positive emotion they seek. However, having a need to be right means you are trying to control or manipulate an outcome through negative actions or words. This will never align you with positive emotion or your true self. When you understand that everyone has their own definition of right based on their experiences, perceptions, thoughts and emotions...then that is empowerment and that aligns you with your true self.

When you give up the need to be right you keep your power. When you keep your power, you are responding from a positive place and your reaction will be one of kindness, tolerance, acceptance and understanding. You realize that you do not need to defend yourself, or be right, in order to feel good. You know that you can feel good regardless of what anyone else is saying or doing. You can let things go quickly and easily with no need to hold onto grudges or resentment. Feeling secure in your thoughts and emotions allows you to remain true to who you are. You are then able to keep your power and react from a place of understanding.

Which reaction feels better to you?

Reacting to someone from a place of understanding, empathy, compassion and acceptance?

Or

Reacting to someone from a place of judgment, jealous, anger or hatred?

You have the power to decide.

What is amazing is, when you choose to react to others from a place of understanding, you are giving them the permission to react to you the same way in return. And…if they choose to react opposite from that, memorize these five amazing words: **It Is Not About Me!**

One of the biggest things to remember before you react to anyone who has "pushed your buttons" (meaning they have pulled you out of alignment into negative emotion) is this: **it is not about you!** Everyone is writing their own story, they are carrying their own baggage, they are dealing with their own thoughts and emotions. All of which you cannot control. Therefore, it is important to remember that if they react to you negatively, it is not about you! If they judge you or shame you, it is not about you! If they talk bad about you, it is not about you! If they lie to you, it is not about you! **It is about them** and you cannot control them. They get to choose their reaction, just as you get to choose yours. If they choose to react to you from a place of misalignment, let that be on them. You get to choose how you want to react; you can choose to respond from alignment; you can choose understanding and acceptance; you can choose tolerance and love. Sometimes all it takes is a quick step away to re-align yourself. Then you are able to react from a healthy place. This is the true meaning of having the power of control.

"Judgement equates to a lack of understanding. Understanding equates to a lack of judgement. Judgement is an inability to show compassion and acceptance to yourself and others. It manifests into negative self-talk and negative reactions towards another. When we accept all of who we are without judgement, we are able to accept others the same."

POWER OF CONTROL
EXERCISES

1. Start by writing "It's not about me." Take some time to write about what that means to you. How will you react differently to people now that you know their reactions are a by-product of their own insecurities, emotional wounds and misaligned thoughts?

_____

_____

_____

_____

_____

_____

_____

_____

_____

_____

_____

_____

_____

_____

_____

_____

_____

_____

2. Make a list of the things you can control and a different list for things you cannot control. After the lists are complete, look for the defining characteristic of each list.

I Can Control

I Can't Control

_____   _____

_____   _____

_____   _____

_____   _____

_____   _____

_____   _____

_____   _____

_____   _____

_____   _____

_____   _____

_____   _____

_____   _____

_____   _____

_____   _____

THE POWER OF ALIGNMENT

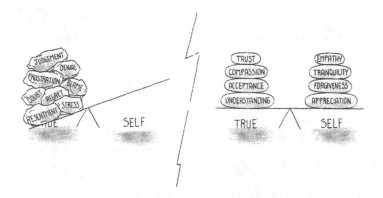

When you are out of alignment with your true self	When you are in alignment with your true self
You feel off or in a funk	You feel exhilarated and ready
You feel exhausted	You feel refreshed and renewed
You feel stress and/or have pain	You feel at ease and healthy
You ignore sensations in your body	You tune into sensations in your body and use them as indicators
You react from an unhealthy place	You react from a place of love and understanding
You blame others or expect them to change	You accept others for who they are
You don't set aside time for self-care	You schedule time for self-care

You are holding onto past hurt and resentment	You have learned from past experiences and let go of hurt and anger
You are carrying grudges from the past	You accept that everything happens for a reason
You want things to be different	You appreciate your past for making you who you are today
You have anxiety about the future	You trust that everything is working out for you
You don't trust the process of life	You look forward to the future with excitement and anticipation
You want to control outcomes	You let go of the desire to be right
You give your power away	You keep your power and act accordingly

Using your Power Against You

You own your power. With this ownership comes responsibility. You must be able to work with your power to keep yourself in alignment. If not, misalignment will occur. Here are a few ways that this can happen.

Wanting a Desire Too Much

We are all given an amazing gift...the power to shape and create a desire and watch it unfold. We have the ability to manifest and live out our dreams. However, having this power can be a double-edged sword. This happens when you use your power to create a desire but then expect it to manifest immediately.

When you want a desire too much, you are using your power against you. The desperate wanting keeps you out of alignment and stuck feeling negative emotion. Fear-based thinking takes over as you concentrate on the *lack* of your desire. The thought of never getting what you want causes you to believe you need to force it into existence. It shadows your ability to allow things to happen and trust in divine timing. You fail to appreciate all you have now because you are too busy looking at what is missing. Ironically, it is focusing on something that is not happening that keeps it from happening; likewise, it is focusing on a problem that keeps the problem active.

You fail to recognize there are two parts in creating a desire, trust and gratitude. Both of which you can only feel when you are in alignment.

It is important to be able to create a desire while appreciating where you are now; thus, being grateful for what you currently have and excited for what is ahead. It is having the ability to keep your desires active while letting them unfold as intended; trusting that everything happens at the perfect time. It is being able to control your thinking into joyful alignment and away from fearful misalignment while you anticipate the unfolding of your manifestation.

Power + Trust, Allowing and Satisfaction
= Alignment and Manifested Desires

Power + Fear, Force and Disappointment = Misalignment and Blocked Desires

Victim of Circumstance

Sometimes things occur in life that make you feel like a victim. Often negative experiences cause you to look for justification as you fail to understand how something so terrible could happen to you.

Remember Olivia whose thoughts held her out of alignment? She was unable to truly enjoy her upcoming experiences because of negative thoughts. Now, what if I added that Olivia's mother died tragically when she was only 15? Because of this difficult event in Olivia's life, she continues to hold onto the negative emotion surrounding her mother's death. Her negative thoughts dictate how she reacts to other experiences in her life. This thinking activates the victim mentality.

Olivia holds onto thoughts that life is hard; that life is not fun or easy. She doesn't think she deserves joy. She believes that if she is happy, she cannot honor her mom. Olivia is using her power against herself. She fails to use her power to shift her thoughts. She uses her power to defend her misalignment because she believes it is justified.

"You must be able to use your power in its purest form. You must be able to work with it, not against it. Each time you work with your power, you are in alignment. Each time you work against your power, you are out of alignment."

How does this happen? Every negative experience is followed by a personal perception. Every person will react differently to an experience. For Olivia, her negative experience created a negative attitude that she believed was justified because of what happened. Other people may become depressed and withdrawn. Some may become angry and lash out or partake in self-destructive behavior. The perception of their experience has caused them to react in a way that they believe is warranted. However, this type of thinking is self-destructive. It will continue to harbor negative emotion and keep you out of alignment.

It is important to realize that everyone has a story. We are not victims; we are participants. Bad things happen to everyone. Every event in your life makes you who you are today and adds to your expansion. Life happens; you can work with it or you can fight against it. It is how you choose to look at every experience that creates the life you are living today.

Giving Away Your Power

When you work to make everyone else happy or protect how others feel, you are giving away your power.

Too often, you worry about upsetting someone or hurting their feelings so you end up doing things that do not align with you. You may go against what you know is right, or what is true to you, because you are too concerned about what others will think.

You give your power away when you believe it is your job to take care of everyone else; to make sure everyone around you is happy. You have a false understanding that if you make others feel good, then you will feel good. However, this ultimately keeps you out of alignment and depletes you at the same time.

> **"Life happens; you can work with it or you can fight against it. It is how you choose to look at every experience that creates the life you are living today."**

When you only know how to please others, you fail to live your own life. You are too busy giving to those around you causing you to neglect yourself. This leads to an empty "well." And, if the behavior continues for too long, you won't even know what brings you joy anymore. You will have lost your sense of self and your true identity.

Graciously giving to others while being able to receive does not deplete. This type of give and take keeps the scale balanced and your well full. Understanding how to say no when necessary is an important part in staying balanced. When there is balance, you are aligned and when you are aligned, you are making authentic decisions. You are able to do things that bring you joy without worrying about the reaction from others.

Staying aligned with your true self and living authentically is vital; learning how to balance your nobility with the ability to receive is key. These skills are essential for living a healthy, joyous life.

> **"When you are in alignment, you are able to connect to yourself, by saying…"**

> **"That thought no longer serves me."**

"It does not fit with who I am today
and the person I have become."

"I am living my own life."

"I make decisions that align with
me. I am true to myself."

"I cannot change that experience. However, I can
change how I choose to think about it right now."

"I will let it play out as intended."

"I cannot force outcomes. It is out of my
hands and not for me to figure out."

"I am at ease letting life unfold."

"I am open to receive."

"I trust whatever is best for me will be."

"I am protected and guided in all I do."

"Where am I right now? This
is what I can control."

"I am safe and loved."

"I appreciate this moment for
all it is bringing me."

POWER OF ALIGNMENT EXERCISES

1. Any word that follows "I am" is the most powerful thing you can say to yourself. Make a list of positive affirmations. Then write them on sticky notes and stick them to your bathroom mirror. Say them aloud to yourself as you start and end your day. Here are some examples: *I am enough; I am strong; I am worthy; I am confident; I am brave; I am loved.*

_____

_____

_____

_____

_____

_____

_____

_____

_____

_____

2. As a way to build compassion and love for yourself, find pictures of when you were a baby or a young child. Put the pictures on your night stand or on the refrigerator. How would you talk to that child? Remember, that child is you, so talk to yourself with love and kindness.

3. Using the t-chart, fill in the columns with experiences in your life when you knew you were in alignment and when you knew you were out of alignment. Compare your lists. What can you do more of that keeps you in alignment with your true self?

In Alignment with
My True Self

Out of Alignment with
My True Self

_____ _____

_____ _____

_____ _____

_____ _____

_____ _____

_____ _____

_____ _____

_____ _____

_____ _____

_____ _____

_____ _____

_____ _____

4. Write about something that pulls you out of alignment. What triggered you that needs healing? What opportunities were presented for you to learn and grow from?

_____

_____

_____

_____

_____

_____

_____

_____

_____

_____

_____

_____

_____

_____

_____

_____

_____

_____

_____

_____

_____

_____

CONCLUSION

Learning how to use the processes described in this book is like healing an opening wound. When your wound is open, it is susceptible to infection. The infection refers to your negative thoughts and misaligned perspectives. This wound is weak and vulnerable. However, as time goes on, and you tend to your wound, it begins to heal. Even though it is still recovering, it is not as susceptible. Negative thoughts may still enter, but not as many and not as often, because a protective barrier is forming. This barrier allows you to catch your thoughts quicker before they penetrate too deep. The wound has gotten stronger and is less vulnerable. When your wound is healed, you are now protected by "little warriors" (positive thoughts) defending your health. When your negative thoughts try to filter in, you can still feel them but they bounce off easily. Your wound has healed. It is healthy, safe and secure. This is you. With emotional awareness, you have the strength to climb up and down the ladder making necessary shifts with ease. You have learned what it takes to stay in alignment with your true self.

When you are in alignment you have found your purpose and your worth. You embrace life with passion. You feel deserving; ready for great relationships and exciting adventures. You know that you do not need to change for anyone and no one needs to change for you. You live with authenticity; proud and accepting of who you are today. You do not care what other people think. You appreciate everyone for who they are and honor where they are on their own journey. You find the value in reacting out of love and kindness. You understand that you are the one who controls every outcome in your life.

> **"Whenever you have a joyful thought,**
> **you have just aligned with your true self.**
> **This feeling of true self is your purpose;**
> **your essence. You are here to participate**
> **in all the good life has to offer."**

When you are in alignment you are empowered with this magic formula. You understand that every thought you think creates your current experience; that you have the power to shape and define who you are at all times.

This discovery leads to the opening of a treasure and finding...

"Who you truly are!"

AUTHOR ENDING

I have concluded through my practice that people don't hear these words enough, so I am telling you now; you are ok; everything is ok; everything will be ok; everything is working out perfectly. It is how you choose to think about it. In order to be part of all the good that is out there for you, you have to believe in the power of you.

Once you find your power, YOU will be the one saying, "I am ok; everything is ok; everything will be ok; everything is working out perfectly for me." And when you believe it and feel it and know it, you have just aligned with you!

As you go forth on your journey through life, remember that you are only a character in other people's stories, you are not the author; don't wait for others to write your story. Go forth and be the author of your own story. Let it be created from a place of understanding, acceptance, appreciation, love and joy. Life is about you and it always will be. Be a joyful creator of your story and let the first words be, "I finally found the power of me!"

Printed in the United States
By Bookmasters